All thanks be to my Lord and Saviour Jesus Christ,
For all His love, grace, guidance and provision.

And to my beautiful and loving wife, Doreen,
For all her love, support and belief in me.

ISBN 978-981-09-1870-5

"To fix a toaster with a loose connection, you don't need to put on display the myriad of hammers, nails and soldering irons that you have acquired over your years of study. All you need is a screwdriver and you need to use it right."

Contents

"All questions share the same building blocks, regardless of topic, factor or discipline. As long as we can decode the building blocks, we can answer any question, anytime, in any discipline."

"It is the Command Word that makes the question, not the content."

"When told to jump, Structured Questions don't ask how high or how far, but how many times."

"What matters is not how many toasters were fixed, but were any of them returned after repair."

"Keep it simple, and answer the question."

Analysing Questions

"All questions share the same building blocks, regardless of topic, factor or discipline. As long as we can decode the building blocks, we can answer any question, anytime, in any discipline."

An important part of exam preparation that is often overlooked is the analysis of questions. The focus of teachers and students is usually placed on acquiring information, forgetting that the content received must be eventually turned into responses which are aimed at answering specific questions.

Without proper guidance, students often end up thinking that questions fit into generic types and there can therefore be a 'one size fits all' approach to answering each type of question. This cannot be further from the truth. Every question is unique. Even if questions look similar, changing one element within the question can change the desired response entirely.

In order to accurately deduce the demands of the question, we must first identify the elements that make up a question.

Here is an example.

Conditional Command Word – Tells you that you can only use information from Figure 2B	Command Word – Tells you that the answer requires reasons to ways (how) and reasons for causes (why)

'Use information from Fig. 2B to explain how and why forests act as Green Lungs of the Earth.   [6]'

Topic – In this case, Natural Vegetation	Factor – In this case, Benefits of Forests	Mark allocated – Tells you that there are 6 reasons for 'whys' and 'hows' in total expected for this question.

From the example, you can see that questions are made up of 6 elements;

1. Topic
2. Section

The area of content to be covered. Different topics have different focus.

3. Factors   The factors/areas to compare/discuss.

4. Command Word   The task which the question sets out.

5. Conditional   The parameters within which the
   Command Word   question is to be answered.

6. Mark Allocation The number of items to be put down.

Let me explain in greater detail the more influential elements.

Command Words

These tell you what the question wants you to do. Typically, there are 1 to 2 Command Words in any question. Care should be taken to identify ALL Command Words so that the requirements of the question can be comprehensively met.

Mark Allocation

It is usually assumed that the mark allocation is evenly distributed across all Command Words. If the question requires a description, an explanation of process or a worked example, the mark allocation will then reflect the number of steps or unique items within the process required in the answer. Therefore, the question in the previous example will require explanations for 3 reasons ('why') and 3 ways ('how') forest act as green lungs.

Conditional Command Word

An often under-rated part of questions is the Conditional Command Word. This refers to any word or phrase that sets the parameters within which the candidate is to answer. It can either look like what has been mentioned in the example, or come in other forms, such as; 'With reference to examples,'; 'Study Fig. 2B,'.

Regardless of how it is worded, the Conditional Command Word must be heeded; else the answer will be void. A deeper discussion can be found in later chapters.

A final element that needs to be heeded is the numbering convention. Questions marked 1, 2 and 3 are discrete and have little to do with each other. Within each question, parts marked (a), (b) and (c) are also discrete and have little to do with each other, save for covering the same topic. However, within each part, sub-divisions of (i), (ii) and (iii) are related, in so far as the answer from (i) may feed (ii) or they may all take answers from the same data source.

Once we have understood the functions of the various parts, we can now begin to classify questions according to broad groups. Here they are in brief summary.

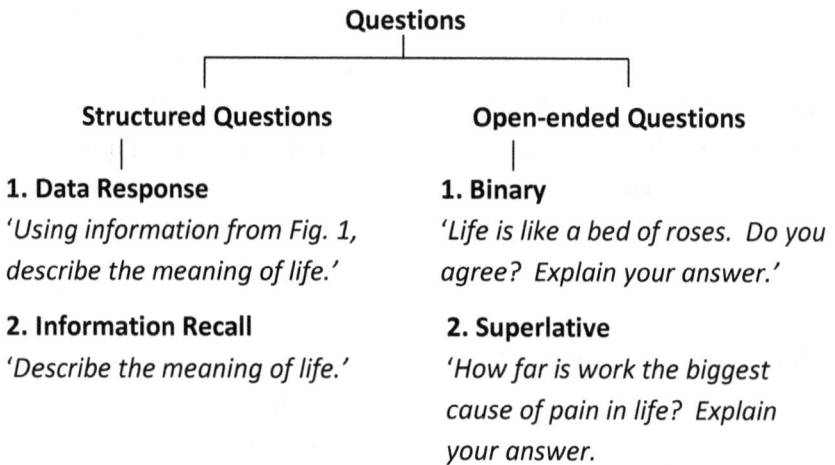

Questions

Structured Questions

1. Data Response
'Using information from Fig. 1, describe the meaning of life.'

2. Information Recall
'Describe the meaning of life.'

Open-ended Questions

1. Binary
'Life is like a bed of roses. Do you agree? Explain your answer.'

2. Superlative
'How far is work the biggest cause of pain in life? Explain your answer.

Structured Questions are those where the **number of marks allocated** corresponds to the **number of times** a task is required to be repeated; or the **number of steps** required in the answer.

Open-ended Questions are those where the **number of marks allocated** corresponds to the answer's **complexity or sophistication**. The marks are usually arranged in levels where the most complex or sophisticated answer gets the most marks.

Amongst **Structured Questions**, the 2 subdivisions refer to;

Data Response Questions which are those where information **is given** and answers are to be derived from the **interpretation of the given information** alone.

Information Recall Questions which are those where information **is not given** and answers are to be derived from **self-study**.

Amongst **Open-ended Questions**, the 2 subdivisions refer to;

Binary – where there are **only 2 sides** to the argument presented.

Superlative – where **the best is to be chosen** from a list of factors. Despite this classification, I am not suggesting that there are generic models that can be used to answer these questions. Instead, each type of question has its own unique demands and marking criteria. Mistaking one for the other will render the answer inadmissible because it does not meet the question's requirements.

Teachers and students alike should therefore be mindful of the role each element plays within the question. By constructing a question in a particular fashion, it sets limits to some aspects and open doors to others and we should be careful to ensure that the question is accurate in conveying the setter's true intent.

In the end, we must understand that the information acquired during study is the tool in the tool box; exam questions are the broken appliances. When fixing a toaster, you don't need to put on display the myriad of tools you have acquired over your years of study. All you need is a screwdriver and you need to use it right.

Exercise

For each of the questions below, answer the questions that follow.

'This coastline often experiences strong destructive waves. Explain why this is so, using evidence from Fig. 1.'   [4]

1. What is the Command Word in this question?
2. Are there Conditional Command Words?
3. Is this a Data Response or Information Recall question?
4. What must the candidate do to get all 4 marks?

'Assuming that the metal is in Group I of the Periodic Table, write an equation for this reaction. State symbols are not required.'   [1]

1. What is the Command Word in this question?
2. Are there Conditional Command Words?
3. Is this a Data Response or Information Recall question?
4. What must the candidate do to get the mark?

'Given that the increase in the cost of a ticket during the peak season is $2.00, form an equation in x and show that it reduces to $x^2-2x-143=0$.'   [2]

1. What is the Command Word in this question?
2. Are there Conditional Command Words?
3. Is this a Data Response or Information Recall question?
4. What must the candidate do to get all 2 marks?

Exercise - Analysis

'This coastline often experiences strong destructive waves. Explain why this is so, using evidence from Fig. 1.'   [4]

1. What is the Command Word in this question?
The Command Word here is 'explain'.

2. Are there Conditional Command Words?
There is a phrase which limits answers to information found only in Fig. 1, "using evidence from Fig. 1". This is the Conditional Command Word for this question.

3. Is this a Data Response or Information Recall question?
While the answer can be conceivably derived from textbook information, the Conditional Command Word dictates that the only information that is admissible in the answer is that which comes from Fig. 1. Therefore, the Conditional Command Word makes it a Data Response.
However, it is worth noting that if the phrase "using evidence from Fig. 1" was removed from the question, it would become an Information Recall question.

4. What must the candidate do to get all 4 marks?
There must be 4 (or more) reasons (as required by the Command Word 'explain') that contribute to the coastline experiencing destructive waves. 4 of them must be given.

'Assuming that the metal is in Group I of the Periodic Table, write an equation for this reaction. State symbols are not required.' [1]

1. What is the Command Word in this question?

The Command Word here is 'write'. Some may mistake the word 'state' to be another Command Word. But taken in context, the term actually reads 'state symbols' which is not a Command Word as it does not give instruction to perform a task.

2. Are there Conditional Command Words?

In this case there are 2 phrases, "assuming that the metal is in Group I of the Periodic Table" and "state symbols are not required". Both these phrases influence the answer, the former limits the group of elements discussed, and the latter prevents the candidate from being penalised for not giving state symbols.

3. Is this a Data Response or Information Recall question?

There is insufficient information in the question to be able to construct the answer. There are also clues in the question that point to it being reliant on prior data. The words **"the** metal" and **"this** reaction" point to an earlier reference or question that helps define to what these words refer. So not only is this a Data Response Question, it is also possibly part of a series.

4. What must the candidate do to get the mark?

Not only does the mark allocation indicate that there is only 1 task to perform, the equation must be expressed flawlessly. If the question had more than 1 mark, that may suggest that the mark scheme delineates method from final answer and so errors in the expression of the final answer will not prevent the student from getting marks awarded.

'Given that the increase in the cost of a ticket during the peak season is \$2.00, form an equation in x and show that it reduces to $x^2-2x-143=0$.' [2]

1. What is the Command Word in this question?
There are 2 here; 'form' and 'show'.

2. Are there Conditional Command Words?
In this question, this is rather straightforward, "given that the increase in the cost of a ticket during the peak season is \$2.00". However, this not so much sets limits to the answer as it gives more information to shed light on the scenario. In short, it paints the picture.

3. Is this a Data Response or Information Recall question?
Given the amount of information that is in the question, it is difficult to tell because all that is needed to answer this question is a definition of how much the cost of the ticket was before the increase. That could have been derived in an earlier question or given in a source.

4. What must the candidate do to get all 2 marks?
2 Command Words and 2 marks suggest that 1 mark is allocated for each of the Command Words. This also indicates that deriving the answer is the only thing that will be awarded with a mark; the method is not awarded.

The Importance of Command Words

"It is the Command Word that makes the question, not the content."

The Command Word is the cornerstone of the question. It gives instruction on what is required. It, together with the mark allocation, gives us the route map to navigate the landscape of the content. Students need to be acutely aware of the fact that it is Command Words that make the question, not the content.

The following is an exercise I often to use to prove this point;
'*List*   the factors influencing Global Warming.'
'*Describe*   the factors influencing Global Warming.'
'*Explain*   the factors influencing Global Warming.'

As you can see, even though the topic, section and factors that the questions deal with are identical, the task varies rather significantly.

In the case of '*list*', the candidate is supposed to identify specific features to meet a particular purpose. There is no need for characteristics or reasons. In contrast, '*describe*' requires candidates to give an account of the distinctive features of the item; while *'explain'* requires reasons for processes or phenomena. Giving one in place of another will render the answer inaccurate to the question. This is true for any subject. Here is an example from math.

'Solve a+b=c'

'Prove a+b=c'

In the first instance, the focus of the question is on deriving the final answer. In the second instance, the focus is on the process of showing the equation to be true.

Various subjects and disciplines have different definitions for what each Command Word means. Teachers and students will do well to get their hands on a copy of their exam syllabus which should spell out the demands and definitions for each of the Command Words.

Nonetheless, Command Words can be broadly classified into 3 types; the *List* type, the ***Describe*** type and the ***Explain*** type.

List
List type questions are characterised by;
- requiring candidates to identify a catalogue of specific features to meet a particular purpose,
- typically brief answers, which could be a short sentence or single word answer.

Other possible terms used to elicit this same response are;
Identify, Name, State, Give, Suggest.

While there are subtle differences between the various forms and therefore different situations for their use, they lead to the same general nature of answer.

Describe

Describe type questions are characterised by;

- requiring candidates to give a written factual account of the distinctive features of an item,
- requiring candidates to relate what an item looks like or to give overall changes and trends.

It is important to note that when used in a Data Response Question, (i.e. questions that require candidates to derive answers from given information) relevant figures should be used to support the description. This is of vital importance as in some subject syllabi, answers to *describe* type Data Response Questions have this requirement inbuilt into the definition of the Command Word and hence, do not earn credit if relevant supporting data is not given.

Here is a worked example;

Question:

'Describe the pattern of daily calorie intake as a measure of food consumption, as shown in Fig 2A.'   [4]

Describe = Descriptor (D) + Evidence (E)

Answer:

'Daily calorie intake is the highest in Australia, with a value of 2901 to 3400 kcal/person.'

It is only when **BOTH** Descriptor **AND** Evidence are present that the answer will merit the 1 mark allocated.

Compare

Following from the *Describe* type question, *Compare* questions are those which build on the same *Describe* skills but double the requirements. Such questions take the elements that make up a *Describe* answer, and add the additional requirement of a comparative adjective between the two descriptions.

Compare may be written as 'List/State/Describe/Contrast the similarities and differences between...' Regardless of the way it is expressed, merely giving 2 descriptions does not make a comparison. The comparative adjective is paramount.

There are 2 ways that such questions can be answered; by grouping the descriptions or by grouping the descriptors. Here is an example worked both ways;

Question:
'Use information from Fig 3A to compare food consumption in Bangladesh and the USA in 2001.'   [5]

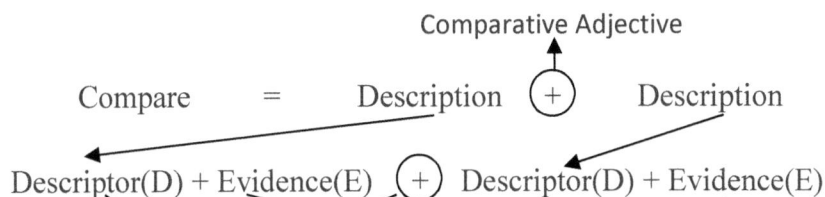

Comparative Adjective

Compare   =   Description (+)   Description

Descriptor(D) + Evidence(E) (+) Descriptor(D) + Evidence(E)

Answer:
'Bangladesh has low meat consumption at 426 thousand tonnes while the USA has high meat consumption at 37551 thousand tonnes.'

OR

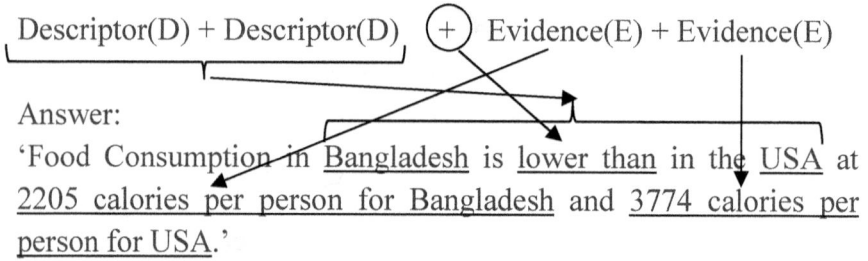

Descriptor(D) + Descriptor(D) (+) Evidence(E) + Evidence(E)

Answer:
'Food Consumption in Bangladesh is <u>lower than</u> in the <u>USA</u> at <u>2205 calories per person for Bangladesh</u> and <u>3774 calories per person for USA</u>.'

Explain

Explain type questions are characterised by;
- reasons provided for the occurrence of phenomena or processes, OR
- short precise definition of terms.

Other possible terms used to elicit this same response are;
For the first type – 'Account for', 'Give/Suggest reasons for'.
For the second type – 'State the meaning of', 'What is meant by'.

This is where the importance of understanding Command Words in context can be clearly seen. This same Command Word, when placed in different situations, elicits differing and mutually exclusive nature of answers.

For example;
'*Explain*   the meaning of Global Warming.'
'*Explain*   the causes of Global Warming.'

In the example above, the same Command Word, when used in the first instance, asks for a definition; whilst in the second instance, it asks for reasons. From here we see the influence that context has on Command Words.

Command Words are also sometimes used in combination. When this happens, it significantly changes the question. Here are some examples;

'Suggest *how* Global Warming has exacerbated.'
'Suggest *why* Global Warming has exacerbated.'

'Describe *how* Global Warming has exacerbated.'
'Describe *why* Global Warming has exacerbated.'

'Explain *how* Global Warming has exacerbated.'
'Explain *why* Global Warming has exacerbated.'

In the first instances (i.e. the *how* questions) the questions focus on the ways global warming has been made worse; and in the latter cases (i.e. the *why* questions) the questions are focused on the reasons for Global Warming.

So when both Command Words are put together, the first instance requires candidates to list ways and reasons, which has worsened global warming; the second instance, to describe the ways and reasons for global warming worsening; and the third instance, to give reasons for the ways and reasons mentioned above. This is yet another example of how Command Words are altered by context.

Conditional Command Word

Complementing the Command Word are words that set the parameters within which the task needs to be completed. These are what I call Conditional Command Words. These can take many forms; 'Using information from Fig. 1,' 'Study Source A and answer the questions.' 'From the graph,' 'Using your answer from part (i)'. This list is clearly not exhaustive.

Regardless of the form, it is clear that Conditional Command Words are usually used to set boundaries to which information for the question can be taken. When used, the Conditional Command Word could potentially pose 3 options for candidates; *can use, must use, must only use.*

Can use
In this case, the candidate has an option to or not to use the information given. There is no penalty if the information is not used. An example of such a question is;

*'Using either information from Fig. 1 **or** your own knowledge, explain the meaning of life.'*

Must use
In this case, the candidate has no option but to use the information given. There will be a penalty if the information is not used. However, the candidate may also use information from his studies, outside of the information given. An example of such a question is;

*'Using information from Fig. 1 **and** your own knowledge, explain the meaning of life.'*

Must only use
In this case, the candidate has no option but to use the information given. There will be a penalty if the information is not used. The candidate also **cannot** use information from his studies. An example of such a question is;

*'Using information from Fig. 1 **only**, explain the meaning of life.'*

We cannot underestimate the importance of Conditional Command Words. By placing such a term in a question, limits are set and therefore answers should not require responses that fall outside of these limits. Similarly, responses falling outside of the prescribed boundaries should also not be awarded.

Exercise

For each of the questions below, answer the questions that follow.

'What factors influence the success of a tourist attraction?'

1. What does the Command Word require in this question?

2. How can the question be changed to elicit a list, a description and an explanation?

'Deduce from the graph whether it was the acid or the marble which was in excess.'

1. What does the Command Word require in this question?

2. How can the question be changed to elicit a list, a description and an explanation?

'If 4 men left after 5 months, how many more months will be required to complete the project?'

1. What does the Command Word require in this question?

2. How will changing the Command Word change the focus of the question?

3. If the Conditional Command Word 'Using information from Figure 1 only,' was added, how would the question change?

Exercise - Analysis

'What factors influence the success of a tourist attraction?'

1. What does the Command Word require in this question?
The Command Word here is 'what'. 'What' looks for nouns, things; as opposed to 'why' which looks for reasons; and 'how' which looks for processes. As such, this question is looking for a list of 'factors' or things that contribute to or hinder the success.

2. How can the question be changed to elicit a list, a description and an explanation?
List – The question already elicits a list, as signalled by the word 'what'. The most obvious alternative to expressing this question is 'List the/Name the/State the/ Suggest factors that influence...'.
Description – Again, the most obvious way to express this would be to use the direct term for descriptions, 'Describe', i.e. 'Describe the factors which influence...'.
A comparison, if desired, may be worded as 'Contrast/Compare the factors which...'. In this case, the focus of the answer changes to the analysis of the factors.
Explanation – The most direct way to change this question is to use the words 'Explain/Account for/Give reasons for/Suggest reasons for'. The focus would then change from merely looking for the list of factors, to eliciting the reasons behind the influence of these factors. Some examiners preface the Command Word 'explain' here with the Command Word 'state' so that the inherent two-fold demands of the question, which are to list and then expound on the reasons are clearer to candidates.

'Deduce from the graph whether it was the acid or the marble which was in excess.'

1. What does the Command Word require in this question?
The Command Word '*Deduce*' requires candidates to make an inference from information given. Therefore, this question requires the judgement, on whether the item in question is an acid or marble, to be based on the information given in the said graph.

2. How can the question be changed to elicit a list, a description and an explanation?
List – To change this deductive question to one that elicits a list, the Command Word '*Deduce*' would have to be changed to a noun, putting the focus squarely on the task of putting down a catalogue of deductions; e.g. 'List the possible *deductions* that can be drawn from the graph.'
Description – Data sources, such as the one that is implicitly referred to in the question as signalled by the words "the graph", lend themselves naturally to descriptive Command Words. e.g. 'Describe the trends shown in the graph.' The limitation is that once the question is changed to a descriptive type question, it would be very difficult to retain the element of deduction.
Explanation – An explanation here could be used to look at the reasons behind the deduction, i.e. 'Deduce from the graph whether it was the acid or the marble which was in excess. Explain your answer.' or 'Explain how the graph helps you with deducing whether it was the acid or the marble which was in excess.' Regardless, the focus would have changed, just like the math example earlier which looked at the difference between 'solve' and 'prove', and now looks at rationalising the answer rather than merely arriving at the final answer.

'If 4 men left after 5 months, how many more months will be required to complete the project?'

1. What does the Command Word require in this question?

The Command Word here is not merely "how" but "how many more months", signalling that what is required is a number, and not a reason.

2. How will changing the Command Word change the focus of the question?

This question essentially requires candidates to derive the answer from a calculation based on given information. There are no items to list, nor describe, nor explain. Therefore, a more fruitful discussion of this question would be to look at the various skills that can be highlighted in a question with this stem.

As it stands, the question is focused on the derived answer. However, if the Command Word was changed from "how many more months" to 'calculate' or 'show', the working would then become important and marks would have to be specifically awarded for the working.

3. If the Conditional Command Word 'Using information from Figure 1 only,' was added, how would the question change?

Similar to the earlier question, this question, as it stands, begs for information on how long it would take if the 4 men did not leave. As such, assuming the required information is given in Figure 1, having it becomes imperative.

Structured Questions

"When told to jump, Structured Questions don't ask how high or how far, but how many times."

The discussion thus far has been on analysing the various components in the question. Now that we have a good appreciation of the functions of the various components, we can look at the nature of various question types.

As mentioned in the earlier chapters, there are 2 types of questions; Structured Questions and Open-ended Questions. We shall begin by looking at Structured Questions.

All the questions covered so far in the exercises and examples are Structured Questions. Such questions have marks awarded based on the number of times the task is being repeated.

Of the 2 types of Structured Questions, we are already very familiar with Information Recall questions. These are the questions that we prepare for by memorising textbook content. We have already analysed these questions in great detail in the earlier examples. Therefore, I would like to look at the Data Response Question.

Data Response questions require students to answer the question **SOLELY** based on information from the data given. There is little students can memorise in preparation for such questions. However, there are still some rules that we can follow to successfully answer such questions. I shall uncover what these rules are by looking at the 2 more popular types of Data Response Questions; the analysis of graphs and charts; and the analysis of distribution patterns.

Analysis of Graphs & Charts

Food Consumption

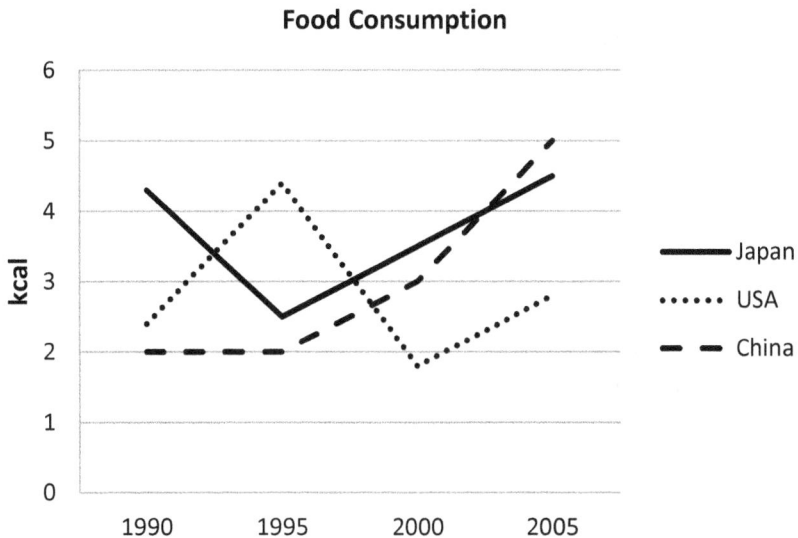

Fig. 1 Food Consumption in Japan, USA and China

The typical question that follows such a graph is either;
Describe and explain the changes in food consumption between 1990 and 2005.   or;
(i) Using information in Fig. 1, describe the changes in food consumption between 1990 and 2005.
(ii) Explain why these changes occur.

Putting aside the fact that the data on this graph is fictitious, we see that in both variations of the question, there are 2 Command Words, '*Describe*' and '*Explain*'. For the '*Describe*' portion of the question, we can find the answer from the graph. That makes it a Data Response question. At the same time, the answer for the '*Explain*' portion of the question is not as readily available and will require book knowledge, so that makes it Information Recall.

Also, the Conditional Command Word '*Using information from Fig. 1*' can only exist if the 2 Command Words of '*Describe*' and '*Explain*' are kept separate. This is because Fig. 1 does not give enough information for an explanation to be formed.

The way to answer this type of question would therefore be to;
- begin with the overall picture
- **then** include individual changes only if they are major exceptions to the overall trend.

The extent to which exceptions should be given is dictated by the mark allocation. Give the first mark to the overall trend(s) and then subsequent marks to the exceptions.

So for this case, the desired description should read thus;
'*Food consumption for most countries remained largely unchanged. This is with the exception of China, which rose.*'

There are 2 general trends given in this answer. That is because there are 2 general trends in the graph. The trend that China exhibits does not fit the trend for their other 2 countries, and hence, there is a need for it to be listed separately.

At this point, we then need to check the number of marks that has been awarded for this question. If the number of marks awarded is

2, then the number of descriptions given above will suffice. However, if there are more than 2 marks awarded, then the analysis will need to go deeper and include the changes within the graph that do not conform to the main trend, such as the rise and fall in food consumption by the USA between 1990 and 2000.

Relevant figures should also be included to support your description. This is especially true for the version of the question which contains the Conditional Command Word *'Using information in Fig. 1'.*

So putting both parts together, we then get the complete answer;
*'Food consumption for most countries remained largely unchanged [**with Japan staying around 4kcal and USA rising slightly from 2.3 to 2.7 kcal between 1995 and 2005**]. This is with the exception of China, which rose [**from 2 to 5 kcal in that time**].'*

The more keenly eyed amongst you will realise that the answer given did not account for the fluctuations between 1995 and 2005. It is not to say that those fluctuations are not sufficiently important to be mentioned, but in terms of priority, the general pattern (i.e. the change between start and end values) takes top priority above all other trends. The other changes should be mentioned only after the general trend has been described, and only if there are more marks allocated for the question than there are general trends.

Trend graphs also lend themselves to *Compare* questions. This is how such questions are usually written;
'Compare the changes in food consumption between 1990 and 2005.'

The way to answer this is similar to the 'Describe' question, except that the comparative adjective should be added and should look something like this;

'*Food consumption for most countries remained largely unchanged [with Japan staying around 4kcal and USA rising slightly from 2.3 to 2.7 kcal between 1995 and 2005] WHILE China rose [from 2 to 5 kcal in that time].*'

Though in this example we are studied a trend graph, this analysis applies to all graphs and charts.

Analysis of Distribution Patterns

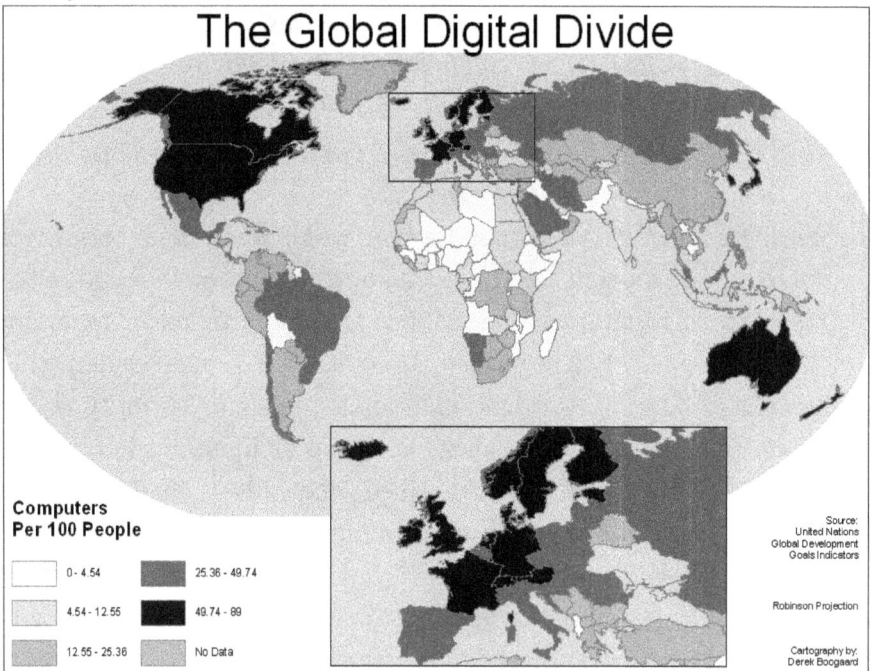

Source: http://upload.wikimedia.org/wikipedia/commons/b/bd/Global_Digital_Divide1.png

Fig. 2 Global Digital Divide according to the UN

The next type of Data Response Question I want to deal with is the distribution question. Their similarity to trend and pattern questions makes them noteworthy for discussion.

Typically, such questions are based on maps or statistical tables. The focus is usually on concentration patterns. Here is an example;
Describe the distribution of computers in the world today.

Similar to answering questions on trends and patters, the way to answer this type of question would be to;
- begin with the locations of high and low concentrations
- **then** include areas which go against the overall trend.

So for this case, the desired description should read thus;
'*The regions with the highest concentration of computers can be found in North America and Canada, Europe and Australia with 49.74 to 89 computers per 100 people. The regions with the lowest concentration of computers can be found in Africa and parts of South America with 0 to 4.54 computers per 100 people.*'

If the question requires a comparison, the case will be similar to the discussion made earlier in the section on Graphs and Charts.

From here we can see that regardless of the material that is given for analysis, the approach is similar, almost identical. And this is really the main crux of this book. Questions share the same building blocks, regardless of topic, factor or discipline. As long as we pay attention to decoding the building blocks, we can answer any question, anytime, in any discipline.

Open-ended Questions

"What matters is not how many toasters were fixed, but were any of them returned after repair."

Open-ended questions take different forms in different disciplines and are graded based on different schemes. Regardless, their common characteristic is that they require the candidate to take a position on a particular concept, idea or perspective and justify the position with evidence. The taking and justifying of a position is the defining difference between an Open-ended Question and a Structured Question.

Amongst Open-ended Questions, there are subtle differences. There are those which offer 2 sides to an argument (the Binary) and those which offer 3 or more factors and require the best to be chosen (the Superlative). Notwithstanding, every Open-ended Question will consist of the following elements:
- a statement which identifies the content and issue to be tested;
- a Command Word that elicits a candidate's judgement and the justification of that judgement.

The evaluative element usually comes in the form of Command Words such as;

- How far do you agree with this statement?
- To what extent do you think/agree that...?
- How true is this statement?
- How successful...?
- Assess the success/effectiveness/impact of...?
- Evaluate the success/effectiveness/impact of...?
- Discuss the advantages and disadvantages of ...
- ... have been viewed as having both benefits and threats. Using examples, explain why this is so.

This list is, of course, not exhaustive but suffice to say that as long as a question asks for an opinion whist comparing factors, situations or causes, it is an Open-ended Question.

Such questions are graded based on various levels of response and these levels are organised with increasing demands on clarity, comprehensiveness and strength or support for the argument. Regardless of the type, the considerations when answering both are the same. This is because the answers are graded similarly.

Personally, I find that the CIE O level geography syllabus offers the simplest and most effective delineation between the levels of complexity and sophistication. Their rubric centres around 3 levels.

Level 1
- Generalised answers generalised with little support.
- Weak reasoning with many parts being unclear.
- Answer has little use of statistics or examples as support for the general argument.

Level 2

- Only ONE SIDE of the opinion is given and supported with appropriate evidence, OR
- BOTH SIDES of the opinion are discussed, with weak support given for either or both.
- Appropriate terms and examples are used with the argument presented in a logical manner.

Level 3

- Comprehensive answers which are supported by sound knowledge of theory and concepts.
- BOTH SIDES of the opinion are discussed and well supported with appropriate examples and evidence.
- Appropriate terms and examples are used with the argument presented in a logical manner and with good expression.

Although different disciplines grade answers differently, almost all Open-ended Answers will be based on these 3 distinct levels. Some may add levels in-between to elicit an even greater level of complexity and sophistication, but few can do with less. Hence, this would, in my opinion, form a good basis for understanding the demands of Open-ended question in general.

With this in mind, there are a few steps that should be followed when writing the answers. Similar to analysing structure questions, we begin by identifying the following items;

Topic ⎤	The area of content to cover.
Section ⎦	Different topics have different focus.
Factors	The factors/areas to compare/discuss.
Command Word	To establish the 2 sides of the argument.

The Command Word for Open-ended questions is particularly important as they define the binary, or the 2 sides of the argument, that is to be dealt with in the question. The terms used to define the 2 sides should be strictly adhered to as changing them can sometimes create inaccuracies in the question. Here is an example; *'Evaluate the effectiveness of international agreements, like the Kyoto Protocol, in combatting climate change.'*

The Command Word here is *'Evaluate'*. However, together with it comes the value term *'effectiveness'*. This term should be strictly adhered to when answering the question. If the term were to be changed to, let's say, *'advantages'*, the subtle difference between an advantage (i.e. to bring benefit) and effectiveness (i.e. the success in producing a desired result) may focus the answer on the opportunities for collaboration that international agreements bring instead on how such collaboration help to combat climate change. This will skew the answer off topic.

So, after establishing the key elements, draw up a comparison table.

	Binary Side 1 (successful, effective..)	Binary Side 2 (not successful, ineffective..)
Factor A		
Factor B		

This table allows for the 2 sides of the argument to be identified and therefore comprehensively discussed in the answer. This is done regardless of whether the question presents 2 sides of an argument or multiple factors for assessment.

Now, we begin writing. Here I would like to offer the following structure as a guide to constructing the answer.

Introductory Paragraph

In this paragraph, you should make the stand should be made explicit and clear. A good start will be to answer the question directly.

Given Factor

Open-ended questions sometimes name factors for discussion. They could comprise all or some of the relevant factors. Regardless, this factor should be dealt with before comparing the factor with other factors. This is how you should write the paragraph.

1. State the point you are trying to make about the factor.
2. Explain what you are trying to say.
3. Give an example or case study to illustrate your point.
4. Say how this affects the question.

Other Supporting Factor (as many as you feel is necessary)

These factors should be handled the same way as your given factor. Follow the steps listed earlier.

Transition Paragraph

After dealing with all the supporting paragraphs, you need to move onto the opposing side of the argument. The point is to acknowledge that there are alternative viewpoints yet be able to persuade the reader that your points are stronger. For this, a transition paragraph is necessary to signal to the reader that you are going to deal with the opposing factors, but not changing your mind about your position. A typical transition paragraph should be short and read like this;

> *However, I acknowledge that there are opposing views to the question.*

Opposing Factor (as many as you feel necessary)
These factors should be handled the same way as your given factor. Follow the steps. The key to these paragraphs is the ending. Though you discuss the strengths in the paragraph, you should state how this factor is flawed at the end.

Weighing Paragraph
This is the paragraph that will set you apart from the rest and move you from Level 2 to Level 3. If done well, this paragraph should be able to show that you have thought through the issue and weighed out the pros and cons of each factor and ranked their importance. You can do this by either grouping the factors by commonality or dealing with them one against the other. But in the end, you should be able to tell the reader which is the most important and which is not. A typical weighing paragraph should sound like this;
Though there are alternative views to the issue, I feel that (whatever you are trying to argue) is still true because... Hence you can see that the main causes are ..., ..., and ..., whilst the other factors, while valid, are not as important to the issue as those mentioned.

Conclusion
Because you have already said so much, this paragraph should be nothing more than restating your stand.

To illustrate the discussion above, here is a worked example;

Question:
'With the use of examples, evaluate the effectiveness of sustainable forest management in maintaining the earth's "green lungs".'

Answer:
Sustainable forest management has been effective in maintaining the earth's "green lungs". Methods such as controlled logging and reforestation have been able to provide sustainable solutions which allow both the use for forests as well as their protection.

[*The response answers the question directly and echoes the term "effective", making clear the candidate's position. The candidate even listed the factors which will be used in the discussion.*]

Controlled logging has been effective as it requires logging companies to extract only the species which they require and not conduct en mass clearing of spaces. This ensures that there will be sufficient vegetation volume to ensure that CO_2 levels are reduced and O_2 levels are maintained. Also, by rotating the plot of land deforested and allowing the area to regenerate, it ensures that the land is given sufficient time to regenerate its forest volume. For example, because of governments such as Brazil and Indonesia requiring loggers to practice selective logging, the pace and hence volume of deforestation has been significantly reduced in these areas.

Reforestation has also been effective in maintaining "green lungs" by regenerating forest volume in deforested areas. Countries such as Indonesia and Brazil have used Agro-forestry to entice logging companies to reforest deforested areas. By creating teak farms in Indonesia and cedar and mahogany farms in Brazil, the respective governments were able to regenerate significant forest volume, for example, in Brazil it was 10,000 ha. This works to ensure that there is sufficient forest volume to effect purification of air.

[*The reasons offered for the effectiveness of controlled logging and reforestation is clear and the focus is not detracted. This is achieved by stating the term "effective" again at the onset of both paragraphs. Relevant examples are also provided and these examples are used to show just why controlled logging is effective. This is something that students often overlook; thinking that mere mention of the place or country would count as an example.*]

However, these methods are heavily dependent on stakeholders conforming to the recommendations of the authorities and laws of the land. This therefore requires comprehensive enforcement to ensure that laws are kept. Developing countries usually have little resource to ensure that corruption does not occur in these countries. For example, in areas as vast as the Amazon and Kalimantan, enforcement is an issue as these governments have limited manpower resources to conduct effective enforcement. Also, corruption, which is rampant in Indonesia, results in logging companies exceeding their logging quotas, while the authorities turn a blind eye.

Furthermore, countries with large tracts of forests are usually developing and would need the use of the natural resource afforded for by the forest and the land on which it stands to fuel its development. As such, there is little motivation for them to police illegal logging in the first place. The net result of these is that vegetation volume is reduced and hence there is insufficient vegetation volume to effectively purify their air.

[*The counter argument mentions little with regard to green lungs but instead chooses to challenge the viability of the methods mentioned before. This works here because the argument hinges on the methods being viable. The examples also work with the argument and show the methods to be inherently flawed.*]

Even though enforcement is a challenge for countries, Agro-forestry builds into itself an innate motivation for companies to engage in reforestation efforts. By turning deforested tracts of land into farmed forests, companies can look forward to a more stable supply of timber for their enterprises. This gives them even greater impetus to ensure that vegetation volume is maintained. As such, sustainable forest management has been effective.

[*The weighing paragraph here puts in place counter-measures to combat the limitations outlined in the section on arguments against. This is what candidates should do here, argue with factors raised earlier and not bring in new information not mentioned, in the hope of gaining more credit. Open-ended questions do not award marks based on the amount of content presented. Rather, it is the quality and comprehensiveness of argument that counts.*]

Notes in Closing

"Keep it simple, and answer the question."

Now that we have a good grasp on what makes up questions, and the different types of questions that are out there, I hope you see the importance that question analysis plays in education. In closing, here are some final tips;

1. **Answer the question directly.**
   It is preferable that you use the words in the question to help you open your answer. This helps you stay on course.

2. **1 point 1 paragraph.**
   This makes it easy for markers to identify the points raised but more importantly, it helps you ensure that you covered the desired number of points.

I hope that this journey in analysis has helped unlock the secrets to understanding and answering questions. As long as we focus on the task at hand and not be preoccupied with showing off the tools we have acquired, we will be able to handle any question, anytime and in any discipline.

www.ingramcontent.com/pod-product-compliance
Lightning Source LLC
Chambersburg PA
CBHW071752020426
42331CB00008B/2284